KALEIDOSCOPE

Terence L. Hanlon

VANTAGE PRESS
New York

Dedicated to Irishtown,
Canso, Nova Scotia

Copyright © 1992 by Terence L. Hanlon

Published by Vantage Press, Inc.
516 West 34th Street, New York, New York 10001

Manufactured in the United States of America
ISBN: 0-533-09728-2

Library of Congress Catalog Card No.: 91-91070

0 9 8 7 6 5 4 3 2 1

These verses were written for fishermen, farmers, laborers, and me.

These poems are not for shouting out
Nor rhetoric their style,
But rather they're soft-spoken
And could evoke a smile!

Contents

Facts

There is nothing quite so springlike
As a morning in the spring
And there's nothing more like songbirds
When the birds begin to sing.

What is grassier than green grass
Or more treelike than the trees?
Who can make a better honey
Than the busy little bees?

The sun gives forth with sunshine
And the clouds are cloudy too.
The sky is always bluer
Than the ordinary blue.

The rains just don't rain flowers,
(Except for just a few)
And there's nothing quite as dewy
As an early morning dew.

All the wondrous things of nature
Are as constant as the sea
But there's nothing as inhuman
As humanity can be.

Prelude to Storm

Blue sea and wide expanse of sky,
In deep and deeper blue horizon merge.
Then floating high, above that placid line,
Bright billow of sun-drenched cloud,
Marches landward, light spurred by gentle breeze.

The graceful gull now soaring high,
Now gliding, dipping low,
His snowy breast and silver-feathered wing
Reflect the sun and flashing in the air,
Bright arcs of light precede the screaming call.

Swell on gentle swell caress the naked coast,
Now rising, swelling high to reach the lighter rock,
And rushing back in whitened foam,
The darkened rock and sand
Its progress marks and holds.

Advancing sea the rugged shore bombards,
Relentlessly to claim its minute gain.
Now gently, now with force of wind and rain,
The battle starts and stops,
With interval of calm and shorter time of storm.

But holds the scene today,
Of clear, calm sky and softly moving breeze.
Mother ocean rests, her heaving bosom,
Unrippled, softly lifts and falls
To lull the coast for future sudden thrust.

To Georgette

Since thou art gone, all life in me
Is like the autumn-nuded tree,
Still living but without a heart
This shell is cold since we did part.

Existing as the wintered earth
Until the sun doth give it birth,
I langour in this semi-life
Awaiting thee, my heart, my wife.

For endless days my being is shorn
Of warmth, from night till cheerless morn
And through the long and empty day,
There's not one sole redeeming ray.

What is the earth without the sun?
What is the game without the fun?
Without my essence which is thee
How dreary can existence be.

Yet must I wait eternally
For that unknown which moveth thee;
But as the winter bringeth spring,
'Tis thee my loneliness will bring.

I wait in knowledge that I may
Regain my heart not long away
And re-awake but never blame
Attracted like a moth to flame.

The Sea of Life

*(Written in 1945 while
at home near the Atlantic)*

O wild and ragged night,
In fury beats your storm
Of cold, cruel wind and rain
'Gainst we frail humanities
Crouched fearful of your wrath.

Stubborn and relentless onslaught
Of hard-driven angry sea
Spurred on in agonized urging,
Impotent to resist your scourge,
Impelling tyrant and sadistic force.

Tossed roughly on your tortured flank
Helplessly drifts the strong-oaked ship
Built well and staunch by skill
Of man's attempted security
From your desperate flight.

O sea that's life and joy
To all that woo thy bounty
Of plenteous fruits and means,
Resist these adverse forces
Of wind and cloud and rain.

Does the nor'west wind come blowing,
O'er the top of "Sally's Hump"?*
And does it slam the cellar door
With a most annoying thump?
Is there still the deep, blue water,
In the harbor and the bay?
And does it change its color
Depending on the day?

When the wind was autumn bitter,
From the north and slightly west,
And the leaves a gaudy glitter,
In that month I like the best.
Just a darkened line in motion,
With an undulating glide,
Waves of eiders skimmed the ocean,
Flowing southward with the tide.

Now's the time to string the tollers,†
While the wind is brisk and cold.
Choose a rock that breaks the rollers,
Like our fathers did of old.
Huddle close behind a boulder,
Just before the crack of dawn.
Press the stock against your shoulder
And suppress that final yawn.

Rowing homeward in the evening,
When the sun-down bunch has flown,
Watching chop within the harbor,
Where the nor'west wind has blown.

*Escarpment at northwest end of harbor.
†Duck decoys.

There's a feeling of redemption
From all the cares of man
And a wish to solve life's problems,
But you're never sure you can.

I have heard there are no porpoise
Like those good old days before
And the sword-fish never ventures
Near the islands off the shore,
And they say the tasty lobster
Is fast becoming rare
And once a year you're lucky
To taste that luscious fare.

Of course I know the answers
But am thinking as I ask
Of how I loved my childhood,
Each pleasure and each task,
From the smell of drying pollock
On the flakes down in the field
To the struggles in the garden
To try and make it yield.

The joys of life are measured
And dispersed throughout one's life,
Depending on the balance
Twixt happiness and strife.
To reminisce of childhood
And things that made it good
Is like kitchen-window gunning*
And eating Mother's food.

*Duck hunting from window facing harbor, outlying, islands, and offshore rocks.

Each season has a memory,
Like gunning in the fall
And hauling up the boats
Before the snow would fall,
Then running on the ice-cakes
In the harbor in the spring,
A challenge to us youngsters
But a most forbidden thing.

And speaking of the seasons
Of the things they bring to mind,
There is one thing kind of special
And exceptional I find,
It was those nights of stories
When the wind was harsh and cold
Of guns and ducks and tollers
When far-fetched tales were told.

These are fondest recollections
Of the not-so-distant past
And in spite of yearly changes,
It's memories that last.
And these are just a sample
Of the lasting things I see
Within my inner vision
Of that town down by the sea.

The seal can leave the ocean
And live upon the land,
The clam can still survive
When taken from the sand.
But in making the adjustment,
There is trauma and there's pain,
And the loss and deprivation
Is far greater than the gain.

Portagee Sam

His face bespeaks an evil heart,
The lines seem hard and cruel.
The beetled brows o'ershade
His eyes of deeply burning fuel.
But deep blue pits like sea or sky
Now troubled, now serene,
On closer scrutiny reveal,
This man's not fierce nor mean.

The toil-bent back and craggy face,
Now fourscore years have stood
And fought the force of wind and rain,
In evil time and good.
Much like the cliffs, down through the years,
He stands unyielding still
And carries on his destined way,
Steadfast and strong his will.

That heart that visage falsely showed,
Is strong and warm and good.
It loved and kindly gave its share,
As much as old Sam could.
The face, unwilling took its form
And like the pummelled coast,
It gave a bit, withstood a lot,
With neither moan nor boast.

Little Tomato*

Little tomato, hop out of my shoe,
Little tomato, I'm talking to you,
Shoes were meant for feet to walk,
Of this I should not have to talk.

If you stay in my shoe this way,
You could get killed most any day,
I'd walk on you and you would bleed
Till all that's left of you is seed.

Hop out and live a little while,
Retain your ruddy skin and smile,
Don't be a sloppy, gooey thing,
Stay round and red and I will sing!

*Written for Laking's daughter when she was six. She found a tomato in her shoe one morning (put there by her father as a joke). She is now a pharmacist in Toronto.

The Trans-Technician*

These are my boys, these rugged men
The back-bone of a station,
In time of need, I must say then,
The life-blood of the nation.

Adept at all the finer things
Like moving things and loading,
At times they even clobber wings
Without excessive goading.

Technician isn't just a name
And this my boys can prove,
Piano-moving is really tame
When they are in the groove.

A grand piano's just a blob
Of wood and keys and legs,
But when my boys have done the job,
There's wire things and pegs.

Aesthetically they re-arrange,
Perfection is their goal,
No longer is the item strange,
They bare its inner soul.

*Air force lingo for "transportation technician." My crew wrecked a piano while loading it on a Herc (transport plane).

The trans-tech has an agile brain,
Of this there is no doubt,
For what he wrongs he rights again,
Repairing with a clout.

Now men who work as I have shown
Must needs have time for cheer
And I am told that they are known
At times to take a beer.

Convincingly I pen this praise
Not doubting you'll agree,
But should you doubt a single phrase,
Your mind is less than free.

South Texas Sportsman

Got a basementful of tackle
But ain't never caught a fish,
But someone saw a mullet
Or was that just a wish?

Now with my lures and tackle
And my truck and trailer joys,
There's my boat and hefty motor,
South Texan fishing toys.

We take off in the morning
With rods and reels and beer,
And we thrash the Gulf 's gray waters
Without a trace of fear.

Of course we're gone at daylight
And we cast and troll till dark,
Then after fifteen bottles,
We thought we saw a shark.

So fishing out of Fulton
Is a much misleading name,
You never get a nibble,
But you can enjoy the game.

It's like picking ripe bananas
In Greenland or in Hell,
But the fishing boats of Texas
Don't have a fishy smell.

The First Ball-Point
(Written in 1940)

I hate a pen that wallows in
The depths of imperfection,
For such a pen is useless then
And plagues me with deception.

It will not write, oh, what a plight
Just when I have a vision,
Idea lost, full out of sight
Must make a new decision.

No use to swear or rant and rave,
I'll simply become pensive,
And now I can my temper save
And pencil down my missive.

Georgia

(Written on my first trip south, in 1959)

It's a way of life the Negro follows,
His philosophy is formed of need.
On the hills and plains and in the hollows
They're left bereft although they're freed.

It seems in every shanty town
That's built of odds and ends
Each dwelling seems to tumble down
With angled pipes and bends.

Each shack is like a crazy quilt
And planning made it so,
It etches in the white man's guilt
And mirrors the Negro's woe.

The white man thinks he's master
Of this sorry backward land
And content to move no faster
Than his shabby hired hand.

He's superior, thinks the white man,
To this dark-pigmented race,
But the only difference is the tan
On his lighter colored face.

So this land of warmth and beauty
Will remain downtrodden still
Till the white man sees his duty
And obeys the good Lord's will.

No matter what your color
Or the texture of your hair,
You may be lighter but be duller
Than a brother not so fair!

A Plea for a Name Change*

I feel a slight confusion
And some degradation too
Has besmirched my reputation
With a name the same as you.
There are galling accusations
And I've heard some whispered words
That a man named J.B. Hanlon
Is strictly for the birds.

Before I moved to MATCOM,†
Your identity was clear,
But now your very nearness
Has created quite a smear.
Old friends who used to greet me
With friendliness and cheer
Mistake me for your grandson
And regard me as a queer.

I have checked your genealogy
Within the Hanlon clan
And have found no trace of *Bertram*
Within our master plan.
It seems some English brigand
Once escaped to Erin Isle
And usurped the name of Hanlon
In a manner bold and vile.

*Continued teasing of my dear friend Bert Hanlon (a WW II hero), merely taking exception to the name Bertram, which appeared a mite English.
†Material Command headquarters of the RCAF.

A damsel tall and sturdy
In Halcyon days of yore
Was a vassal of our Chieftains
And the clan's outstanding whore.
To protect her from the peasants
And to keep her loyal and tame,
She was granted in her childhood
The protection of our name.

So when the beast from Britain
Came to soil the Emerald Isle,
He seduced the family harlot
And commenced your rank and file.
This is not to call you bastard
Or refute your claim to fame,
But there's something underhanded
In the way you got your name.

I'm not one to sneer at peasants
Nor to criticize your kind,
But denying I'm related
Is becoming quite a bind.
Now I offer this solution
As a *true* O'Hanlon man,
Could you now become *O'Houlihan*
To purify our clan?

First Impressions of Florida

Now Florida is the Sunshine State
True natives will relate
And if it rains from morn to night,
It's just precipitate.

There's never wind and never cold,
They'll swear cocksure and bold,
And though the temperature is low,
It's merely cool, I'm told.

No citrus fruit can quite compare
With oranges or grapefruit fare
And if you get a sour orange,
It wasn't grown down here.

So if you find it cold and wet
Or even foggy yet,
It's not the climate of the state,
It's just the folks you've met.

The Brewmaster
(*My friend Ozzie's venture into home-brewing*)

Down through the years he brewed his beers
Of malt and liquids potent
And though he showed the wears and tears,
He kept his high "I" quotient.

Still not content could Oscar be,
He brewed a stronger nectar
And tried it on his wife to see—
The damned stuff nearly wrecked her.

So now he knew he had a brew
Was fit for gods or devils,
This newest brew was light as dew,
In new-found joy he revels.

The corn-meal mash became the key
To this new bright elixir,
But from his looks, if you ask me,
Oz soon will need a mixer.

Still not to sway him from his way,
He utilized his corn-mash
To make a golden Johnny cake
And ate it with his spud-hash.

A feast for kings it proved to be,
He numbly felt but could not see,
O snakes and gremlins on the wall
Who hit our Oscar with a mall?

Our Beloved Air Vice-Marshal

The parade was drawn in line precise,
Each man his stance was rigid,
With stature straight and eyes like ice,
Their feet and hands were frigid.

The AOC, the dais gains
Then turns and grins with pleasure,
His gallant men return the grin,
"The boss he is a treasure."

Infectious smile of AVM
Has warmed the coldest rebel,
Entire wing from flight to flight
Bend forward, back and treble.

Relaxed and warmed in line they form
And march past in a jumble,
They grin and grin and eye the boss
Not even sergeants mumble.

The Candidate

With clammy palm and feeble wrist,
He shakes my hand and mumbles "How."
His smile is but a timid twist
Of pallid face and wrinkled brow.

He faces me with vacant stare,
Not knowing that his soul is bare
And mumbles incoherent words
In language strictly for the birds.

Just one more hulk with pointed head
Whose heart is slack and mind is dead,
Without a spark of human wit,
Can't even think a little bit.

I feel depressed with full dismay,
How could a person get this way?
But hold it!—one must be observant
He's qualified as Public Servant.

The Birdwatcher

Behold him single in the field,
Or crouched beneath a tree.
He isn't hiding from the world,
He merely stoops to see.

His mind is taken up with birds,
Alert are all his senses.
He searches for them everywhere,
Along the trees and fences.

No hunting dog did ever strain,
With keener sense of duty.
His object's not to trap the prey,
But merely view its beauty.

From constant straining he's become
Much like the timid deer
And with his watching duties done,
He hurries home in fear.

See how his head comes to a point
And how his back is bent,
How setterlike his drooping ears,
To hear just where they went.

Politically his mind is free,
His creed is not in words.
He neither holds to right nor left,
He's strictly for the birds.

The Pecan Way

I travelled down through Georgia state
On a bright and sunny day,
Each mile I passed just made me hate
The well-marked "Pecan Way."

On every turn both left and right,
An ugly billboard stood,
Deleting scenery from my sight
Proclaiming pecan food.

There are pecan pies and pecan rolls
And pecan custard too,
There's even pecans made with holes,
I'll bet there's pecan stew.

Your eyes are filled with pecan signs,
There's naught else you can see,
They're guaranteed to crack the minds
Of folks like you and me.

So just to please my mental urge
And free me from the rut,
I fell in with the pecan surge
And found it's just a nut.

Sportsman Manor
(Our winter refuge in Rockport-Fulton, south Texas)

They call it Sportsman Manor,
But why, I'll never know,
For evidence of sporting
Most surely doesn't show.

Perhaps it is a sportsman
Defined as, "one who will,
Dream of fish and ocean
When he takes a sleeping pill."

And the ad will mention fishing,
And a "lighted fishing pier."
But should one go a-fishing,
He'll never catch one here.

And of course there is the statement
That there is a swimming pool,
But one who dives within it
Would have to be a fool.

There just ain't any water,
But there surely is a pool,
But a pool that's lacking water
Was not defined in school.

Ode to Ale*

O effervescent liquid divine,
Not comparable to whiskey or wine,
All I know is you are mine,
Which is fine.

O soother of conflict and emotion,
I would that you composed the ocean,
Gentle coolant, tender lotion,
What a potion!

O Molson, Dow, Labatt and Dawe,
I sing your praise in reverent awe,
Your art is fine, there is no flaw,
To you—Hurrah!

O amber ale, some dark, some pale,
If I drink too much, I'll end in jail,
Sudsy, frothy, stout and hale,
Hear my wail.

O snakes and gremlins on the wall,
Did someone hit me with a mall?
The floor beneath doth rise and fall,
I fear that's all!

*St. Francis Xavier University English class project, 1939, chosen
by Professor Dickie Bannon to read before the class.

The Slug and the Escargot*

The slug and the escargot
Are very much the same,
In fact they only differ
In their costume and their name.

One is just a little fatter
And enclosed within a shell,
The other is more open
But considers work is hell.

The slug, of course, is sluggish
And escargots aren't too fast,
But they have a common heritage
In occupations past.

They both were trained in uselessness
And with honors passed the course,
Then after graduation
They enlisted in the force.

The escargot was contented
To remain upon the ground,
But the slug, in spite of sluggishness,
For higher things was bound.

*Two fellow officers with the RCAF in France—Station adjutant S/L
(escargot) and Station protocol officer S/L (slug), 1962.

So the slug became a pilot,
Which proves what I contend
That any breathing creature
Could be one in the end.

The slug at last is grounded,
The escargot forged ahead,
One rests beneath his ugly shell,
The other stays in bed.

The Officers Mess; or, The Wax Museum

*(The RCAF headquarters mess in Ottawa—
revisited many years after World War II)*

This was once a place of revelry,
Like knightly halls of old,
Where bold men became normal
And timid folks were bold.

No more the sounds of merriment
Or youthful voice in song,
To laugh or shout or frolic
Is now considered wrong.

No more the shining faces
With exciting, lively talk,
It is almost sacrilegious
To move or breathe or walk.

Now the forms in many poses
Are inanimate and old
And the pallor of their faces
Spreads an aura stern and cold.

And the drinks once raised mid clamor
With a shouted toast or jest
Now stealthily are voided
With a dribble down the vest.

When the spirit leaves the body,
Like a light from out the room,
There is not a sound or glimmer
In the all-pervading gloom.

The Snow-Bore*

The Snow-Bore plods his weary way,
Through tons and tons of snow.
He's like a glow-worm in the day—
He just ain't got no glow.

Nobody sees this little thing,
Though he comes up for air.
He's like a smeagle on the wing,
Invisible, but there.

He bores a hole and pulls it in,
Behind him as he goes,
There's not a trace of where he's been,
When sought by friends or foes.

We know he is but think he ain't
Around us when he's gone,
But like a light that wasn't lit,
It hardly could have shone.

*The Snow-Bore is common to any area where there is snow. Although not detectible by human senses, they're there, but you have to take my word for it.

Scrambled Gum-Boots*
*(Written shortly after President Kennedy's
assassination)*

Why is a tree?
And how do squirrels?
And clouds are cloudy too.
Dandelions are dandy,
But malt's a better brew.

The grassy grass
Is grassier than moss
And song-birds sing.
The earthy earth is dirt.
Now that's a funny thing.

H bombs and Bomarcs
And blondes and brunettes too.
Summit men are tops,
Fish are fishy things
And beer is made of hops.

Satellites and sputniks
And cranberry sauce.
Governments are dead
And dew is damp.
The whole world needs a head.

*With apologies to "Fried Shoes," written by an American poet.

Son of the Victors*

"Son of the Victors" marching on
With your white flag flying high,
There's none to tell your secret dark
And none to ask you why.
When Cromwell fought your chieftains
And put your clan to rout,
He left them but a boar's head
And one bedraggled goat.

You're the last surviving remnant
Of a once commanding clan
Because you used discretion
And instead of fighting ran.
The boar's head was your dinner
With an apple for dessert
And the goat's skin, worn and shabby,
Has served you as a skirt.

Now in the halls of heraldry
Emblazoned on a shield,
Your escutcheon is a boar's head
On a fleecy goat-skin field,
And if you need a tartan
To commemorate your fight,
Why not a yellow ribbon
Down your waving flag of white?

Terence Leonard McSweeny *Smith.*

*Kidding my good friend Bertram Hanlon after a discussion of the
Hanlon genealogy.

The Tobacco Addict

Look at his dim and jaundiced eye—
His stained and shaking finger.
With tar-gummed lung and tattered heart
Who knows how long he'll linger?

And from his mouth a smell like hell,
Of brimstone, smoke, and ashes,
His tortured lungs recoil and ache
As if from many lashes.

Outward Bound

Sleek hull from stem to stern,
Tall spars and canvass white,
Quick tacking makes her turn
With jumbo full and mainsheet tight.

Quick on the scudding wave,
She darts before the wind.
Her keel the blue depths shave,
Tall masts straight forward bend.

The *Lunenburger* outward bound,
The Grand Banks are his goal,
He'll search the brine 'til fish are found
In ocean deep and shoal.

Retrospect

Oft I have lain
In the warm sunshine
Where the breakers roll
With their spray of brine.

In their phantom race
Across the sand,
They gently bathe
The peaceful land.

The murmur of
The surging swell
Oft broken by
Some harbor bell.

That great blue bosom
In rhythm swelling
Nurtures all life
Within her dwelling.

The swordfish, lobster,
Crab and whale
Cavort and play
Beneath her veil.

A great deep mystery
Is the sea.
It oft takes life
But pleases me.

The Gannet

He poises on his pedestal of air,
His flashing wings retain
The spot from which to launch
His boltlike thrust
And snatch the fish below
From life to sudden death.

Our Insignificance

Indifferent act
May wipe out life
And make a widow
Of some wife.

For just as we
May squash a fly,
Fate will not always
Pass us by.

The ant, unthinking,
Builds his hill
Oblivious to
The human's will.

Just as the ant,
We too must be
Quite ignorant of
Life's destiny.

In the vast scheme,
As days go by,
We mean no more
Than the common fly.

Don't brood too much
On present sorrow,
For you may never
See tomorrow.

So breathe life's air
While still you may,
Live, laugh, and love
From day to day.

The fate that swiftly
Dispatched the fly
Can in an instant
Demand you die.

Nora

(*1958—a niece*)

A sunbeam with a body
Made brighter, clearer still,
A bubbling piece of happiness
A rainbow seems to fill.

Cheeks like pansy petals,
Eyes that flash with purest light,
Ruby lips and teeth of whiteness,
Framed by hair of darkest night.

She's the essence of perfection,
Like the sun's first beaming ray,
The most beautiful of women
And she's five years old today.

Spring
(*Spring of 1953*)

The dandelion, the buttercup,
All verdure forthwith springing
Don once again their gaudy train,
Their share of rainment bringing.

The stage now set, the birds and bugs
Rehearse melodious greetings,
Their hearts are free in stump and tree
For peaceful, amorous meetings.

Enjoyments still by beauty fill
The heart that once was aching,
There's more to life, there's more to love
Than giving it and taking!

Youth

In youth all motivation is
From dreams of future living
The stress is strictly on the get
And never on the giving.

Insignificance

Imprisoned on this island globe
From all that endless space,
A speck upon a spot am I
And all the human race.

One grain of sand upon a beach
Unknown, completely lost,
The universe beyond my reach,
By shifting winds I'm toss't.

Though insignificant my lot
And ignored is my existence,
I cling to life with just one thought:
What causes this persistence?

The Wind

(1986, Irishtown)

I love to wrestle with the wind,
And feel its clutch and grasp.
It pulls my hair and bends my back
And makes my breathing rasp.

And leaning forward 'gainst its force,
I slowly stretch its hold . . .
And panting feel a warmth within,
Although its grasp is cold.

From warming hold in summertime
To winter's chilling blast,
I try to break each grip and clutch
But make the contest last.

Like yielding only partly
To life's annoying ways,
One can enjoy the struggle,
Be it for years or days.

Thoughts
(1957)

Who marries and begets a child
Should not forget the urge is wild.
'Tis nature planned ignoring thee,
Nor more required than a tree.

But as the tree maintains its seed,
So must the human care and feed
And nurture them until full grown,
But after that they're not their own.

There is some high and mighty force
Which guides the stars within their course,
'Tis known as nature or as God
And forms the seed within the pod.

No human being can quite conceive
Those wonders that his eyes perceive,
In ignorance he thinks he's first,
Why drink when one has not a thirst?

Each one a purpose has in life,
Perchance a husband or a wife,
Which role they play is never known
'Til course of life their way is shown

The acorn knoweth not the tree,
Thy children oweth naught to thee,
In nature's plan your role was filled,
'Twas not by you your life was willed.

The Hypocrite

The merchant toils week in and out
And only thinks of money
And how he keeps his record clean
Of sin is really funny.

The better part of all his life
He works for worldly pleasures,
But once a week he's sure to seek
A blessing on his treasures.

When Sunday comes he changes to
A repentant minor sinner
And dedicates his life to God,
At least before his dinner.

Now off to church with solemn step,
His pious face enraptured,
Today he is a Christian man,
Real saintliness he's captured.

The congregation looks and smiles,
His position they admire,
Although they know the merchant
Is a cultured thief and lair.

For six of seven days a week,
He steals and cheats his neighbor,
But on the seventh he will seek
The church to bless his labor.

He firmly thinks religion is
An antidote for evil
And like a spray applied to plants,
The potion kills the weevil.

The Inevitable

He's old and lost and hurt inside,
His faltering steps the young deride,
There's not a face he'll recognize,
No friend remains to sympathize.

Last year he was a part of life,
He had his job and still his wife,
But now retired, bereft of spouse,
There's nothing but an empty house.

His children know that he's secure,
But money never was a cure
For loneliness when one is old,
Care is warm, neglect is cold.

There's just a few of life's years still,
Why must they be so hollow?
You'd think that youth the void would fill,
They know they're bound to follow.

Rebirth

And once the cold, clear days subside,
The breath of May her living germ
Into the world her seed disperse
In all-embracing, flowing life,
Her breast is warm.

The coming of the Springtime
The resurrection of the dead,
The lifting of the blanket
From earth's chill-darkened bed.

Unfettered spring the brooklets,
The rivers and the streams
In joyous, sparkling freedom
To live their winter dreams.

They flow ecstatically along
To dampen earth's cold hardness,
They fill her veins, revive her heart,
Renew her fields with gladness.

Whither Lions and Christians

I was walking near the Rideau*
When a fearsome sound I hark,
A sound of frightful frolic
From a place called Lansdowne Park.†
Within my heart a feeling
Twixt curiosity and fear,
A brief and sudden battle fought,
And then I found me there.

Methinks the days of ancient Rome
Presented such a sight.
The greensward and arena gay
Quite flooded out my fright.
Like on the feast of Lupercal,
The raucous mob besat,
I drank in the excitement
And forgot where I was at.

A wondrous sight besmote my eyes
Of folk in bright array,
As vivid as the northern skies
When winter's on the way.
Full thirty thousand filled the stands,
From senator to pleb,
And even staid, reservèd souls
Were caught up in the web.

*River flowing through the city of Ottawa.
†Football stadium.

Opposing gladiators stood,
Betwixt them paces three,
And armed with naught, though armored light,
They crouched and glared with glee.
An odd-shaped bag of skin and air
Was clutched close to the sod
By one, who though indeed a slave,
Showed stature of a god.

A deafening silence filled the air
With not a thing to hark,
A tribute to the Leaf and Crown
By all within the park.
Why hold they to two major gods?
Of this I have no clue,
But it would seem great Juppiter
Divides their faith in two.

Before the rugged battle starts,
The jesters intervene
In stripèd tunics, black and white,
To humorize the scene.
They ham and clown and foollike act
To mitigate the tension.
Apart from this their usefulness
Is really not worth mention.

A sudden shriek the silence cracks,
From whistle, flute or horn
And what was fragile silence now
By raucous roar is torn.
The factions urge their champions on
And scream for strife and blood,
From flailing feet and gouging knees,
The turf has turned to mud.

Beneath the screaming watchers,
On the south side and the north
Appear to be two noblemen
Fast pacing back and forth.
To me it seems their purpose
Is apparent from their mien,
They're there to see no combatant
Escapes the battle scene.

Now as the battle quickens
For that bouncing bag of skin,
A gleam of understanding
Begins to flood my ken,
Those agitated gentlemen
Beneath the screaming knaves
Are the leaders of each faction
And commanders of the slaves.

Quite oft a gladiator
Sore wounded and in pain
Is quickly patched and mended,
Then forced to fight again,
But when no longer able
To keep up with the pace,
He is carried from the melee
And another takes his place.

Now in those days when Christians
Formed the entertaining teams,
No need was found for medicine
Nor a trainer's skills, it seems.
Convinced that their salvation
Required they be killed,
They glimpsed the way to paradise
And kept the bleachers filled.

Perhaps a modern "Red-top"*
Could accomplish quite the same
If he billed an execution
For each and every game.
The victims would be members
Of the cablevision team,
A cheap and certain method
To realize his dream.

For sixty solid minutes
The battle ebbed and flowed
And in the autumn freshness,
The screaming faces glowed.
Then in the final minute
With seconds running out,
The stronger gladiators
Put the other team to rout.

And maddened by the battle
The mob broke through the stands
And spilled upon the greensward
With eager grasping hands.
I know not what their purpose
Nor would I care to guess,
But I'm glad I wasn't costumed
In gladiator dress.

*Former player and manager of the team.

Each era has its outlet
For the daily strain and stress,
Whether watching gladiators
Or observing mini-dress,
But this spectacle at Landsdowne
When it's lovely in the fall
Is a throwback to the Romans,
But the greatest of them all.

So despite the sight of mayhem
And the fearsome things you hark,
There's a cure for killing boredom
In a place called Landsdowne Park!

Coach and Martyr

*(The Coach of the Ottawa Rough Rider football team
    in the late 1950s)*

They howl in fury when we lose,
They mumble when we win,
They're long on judgment, short on clues,
Their loyalty is thin.

Admittedly they pay the price
To rant and blow off steam,
But constant moaning isn't nice,
It doesn't help the team.

That haggard, weary, ulcered man,
The object of their wrath,
Although he does the best he can,
He treads a thorny path.

His worries mount to more than just
The coaching of the team,
To please the fandom is a must,
Essential it would seem.

So when he's won a game or so,
The baying hounds are still,
But when he drops two in a row,
They clamor for the kill.

His stipend may in one short year
Amount to quite a sum,
But he is worth it, never fear,
This hero and this bum.

An Act of God; or,
Leo's* Lament

It seems the place for oracles,
Is not within a team,
Their job is work and practice
And keeping on the beam.

An "Act of God," he stated,
Is what the Riders need
To ever edge the Argos,
But Riders paid no heed.

Now Clair is not a prophet
Nor deity or such,
But he and his commandos
Thought Leo talked too much.

So Jackson, though a mortal
(In spite of what they say),
Decided with his cohorts,
This really was his day.

Of course there were the angels
Like Billy-Joe and Shirk,
Much needed by the master,
To make the magic work.

*Leo was a former Toronto Argo coach who stated that only an act
of God could prevent his team beating Ottawa in the play-off.

And in that host of angels
Were many names that shine so true,
Like Poirier and Joyner
And Gaines and Lehman too.

But in an act so perfect,
There is need for many souls,
Like all of those defenders
With one who misses goals.

With spirits like Tom Beynon
And Perdrix and his mate,
The forward saints or sinners
Kept Argos from the gate.

More spirits in the back-field
Like Wayne and little Ron
Kept scoring points like demons
And putting Leo on.

In thoughtless desperation
Poor Leo spoke those words,
But his psychologic efforts
Were strictly for the birds.

Allowing that the Riders
Are not a Godly lot,
The Act comes as he called it,
But much worse than he thought.

To Abercrombie

Dear Ab, you clowning hunk of mirth,
Your jokes are corn from out the earth,
In spite of this I like your kind,
You figment of the master-mind.

Don't misconstrue as flattery
Each last line of this battery,
Sometimes you miss but still you try,
The credit always goes to Lye.

You minstrel, actor, prophet too,
There's much in what you say, is true,
But when you act or when you sing,
The puppeteer must pull the string.

A team you choose because you must,
A local station must be just,
How fortunate it is the best
Or Lye would never pass the test.

Predictions are not always right,
But when a team shows so much fight
As Riders manifest of late,
Lye is an accurate running mate.

So, Ab, just call them every game,
The other teams will soon be tame,
The Argo bubble soon will burst
And Riders yet will end up first!

Ron Stewart—the Human Sidewinder*

The stature of a man
Is not measured by his girth,
Nor do his height and weight
Determine what he's worth.
It's the engine that's within
Gives the power to a car
And it's courage and it's heart
Makes a man a football star.

He is small but he is mighty,
A dynamic driving force,
A diminutive young Atlas
Though he never took the course.
The most stubborn opposition
Strives to put him to the test,
But he foils their every effort,
Gamely proving he's the best.

Running, blocking, catching passes,
Up the middle, round the end,
He can take the hardest tackle
And he doesn't even bend.
He's a compact little package,
Strongly muscled, keen of mind,
On his own or with his blocking
He just leaves them all behind.

There is none exactly like him
Quite so fearless, strong and bold,
When the Lord had made Ron Stewart,
It appears he lost the mold.

*A small but outstanding offensive half-back with the Rough
Riders.

Contemplation by Frank Clair*

A football expert is a clot
I very much admire,
He picks us last of all the lot
Each year—he'll never tire.

This way we know just where we stand,
Our only move is up,
Considered last in all the land,
We still could take the CUP.

In June the expert feels quite free
And rates us all by ear,
He quickly writes off Bill and me,
Though him we haunt each year.

So once again it's playoff time
And now we get a cheer,
'Til now they'd never bet a dime
We'd be around this year.

*A very successful head coach of the Rough Riders.

But still I say we like it best
To be forgot each year,
And even when we face the west,
The experts shed a tear.

There's Dixon, Shatto, Henley and
The stars of all the rest,
But never mention of the band
That proves they are the best.

We unknowns still will carry on
And just could take it all,
The experts then will all be gone
'Til canning time next fall.

In Memoriam

Poor Jungle Jim* he stands aghast
With pistol to his head,
His team is done, their rule is past,
He might as well be dead.

His clawing cats have lost their nails
Against Rough-Rider steel,
His voice is gone, his visage pales,
His fans call him a heel.

If Jim had bit his tongue so loud
And kept his peace of mind,
His fans might stay upon their cloud
And treat big Jim more kind.

But Jungle Jim so arrogant,
Just made the Riders sore,
Of dirty play they're tolerant,
But Jim was such a bore.

So, Jim if you are still alive,
Take this bit of advice
On prophecy a team can't thrive
And bragging just ain't nice.

*A very outgoing Hamilton Tiger-Cat head coach.

Tigers to Tatters in 120 Minutes

(Final play-off game, in which Hamilton was badly beaten by Ottawa)

Some weeks before Christmas
The holocaust came
And wiped out the Bengals
In spite of their name.
Old tigers were kittens,
Quite meek and demure,
For the *Rough* in the Riders
They couldn't endure.

For years they survived
Just by dint of their luck,
But when their time came,
They hadn't the pluck,
Their spirit was broken,
Their muscles were frayed,
Defence was just token
While Sazio* prayed.

Old blubber-gut Mosca
Was slower than slow
And he asked dazed and battered—
"Which way did they go?"
Disdainful the Riders
Kept him down in his rut
As they ran through and over
His big, beefy gut.

*Hamilton team manager.

Poor Barrow was once
A real hunk of a man,
But in front of the Riders,
He flopped on his can,
And the great Billy Ray
Was kittenish too
As the tackles he made
Were feeble and few.

Now poor old prince Hal,
Once a peach of an end,
Had slowed to a crawl
(For he's way round the bend)
And poor Garney Henley,
Their only bright light,
Found himself quite bereft
Of all aid in the fight.

With great indecision and panicky pains,
Big Joe and Frank threw
For Rough Rider gains.
Each time that he scrambled
And pointed his nose,
He saw only players
In Rough Rider clothes.

Now the nights will be long
And the days will be cold,
For the last of the tabbies
Are beaten and old,
All hope for the future
In Tiger-Cat town
Can be seen in the sadness
Of Sazio's frown.

**Man with an Idea;
or,
The Culmination of Oscar's Mental
Processes**
(*For my dear friend Major/General Oscar Hardy, who
commenced service with my section in Ottawa as
a young Flying officer*)

Vesuvius fumed and spewed her wrath,
Olympus showed the Gods their path,
On Calvary stood salvation's hill,
And Carter made the liver pill.

But all of this is now consumed,
A brilliant light a dome illumed,
To speak is verbal diarrhoea
Oscar conceived his first *idea*!

I'm Cured*

The medical profession
Is a complicated thing,
There's a specialist for the intake
And a specialist for the ring.

If you feel you want a doctor
And examination need,
Be prepared to take a beating
That will put you off your feed.

At least four will gather round you
With bright sadistic eyes,
They will pummel, prod, and jab you,
Then swear you're telling lies.

They will diagnose your trouble
In their weird and wondrous ways
And even if it's minor,
You won't feel the same for days.

If you're sure you have a pain
In the tummy or the back,
It still could mean your noggin
Is completely out of whack.

*After a medical by six-foot, T-shirted, cigar-smoking L/Col.
Powell (chief surgeon) and his cohorts, 1960.

For you are just the patient,
You can't really know what hurts,
You may still have corns or bunions
Though your heart just works in spurts.

A throbbing in your ear drum
Could mean your liver has to go,
There is even halitosis
In the nether parts below.

When the biggest and the roughest
Bares his finger—then you're had,
And you feel just like a rocket
On a vicious launching pad.

But of one thing I am certain,
When they've put you through the mill,
You will ne'er again approach them,
Not even for a pill.

Up or Down

It seems today in football games
Psychiatry is needed,
The coaching staff have psychic names
For players they have weeded.

Potentially a man can be
A Jackson, Vaughan, or Thelan,
But coaching staff can plainly see
He lacks that prideful feeling.

Psychology a jumble is
Of psychic ins and outs
And is a major portion of
A football coach's notes.

The human beings that make a team
Will change as tension mounts,
But whether lax or full of steam,
It's up or down that counts.

Explaining for a losing team,
All coaches say the same,
They played their best but lost because
They weren't up for the game.

Now *up* is quite descriptive,
It means a team is hot,
And *down* is just a cover-up
For all the things they're not.

70

But what is quite confusing
To us football fans and such
Is when they're down they're only down
But up can be too much.

They must be up, but not too far,
For this could make them tense,
Their endocrines must level off,
It's only common sense.

So if perchance a coach could tell
His team is just too up,
Would tranquilizers used with care
Ensure they win the cup?

Curable Malaise

(The Canadian constitutional controversy)

O Canada, you crippled tortured thing,
So sick within, proud osprey without wing,
Opposing forces in your being flay,
Your soul and heart in never-ending fray.

O vision, which from birth was ever bright,
What illness from within obscures the light?
Some virus in the blood now dims the eye
And makes you, yet so young, appear to die.

Oh, wither now, physician with a cure,
Some diagnostic marvel true and sure,
To find and purge the poison from your head
And save you from that fate we dreamers dread.

Lost causes give the challenge to the strong,
The patient use of wisdom rights the wrong.
Cannot the learnèd mind resolve the why?
There must be one, at least could make a try.

Perhaps what seems completely lost,
Could be retrieved without excessive cost.
Return our once unwavering belief,
Cross-pollinate the Lily and the Leaf.

Appendix

POEM IDENTIFICATION

During the course of these verses one may encounter poems "to Ozzie" or some that refer to "Bertram." In any case, the first refer to my very good friend Ozzie Hardy (RCAF retired), the other to another good friend named Bert Hanlon, no relation that I know of, but a great friend and a World War II hero in the RCAF (Royal Canadian Air Force). Some references to my RCAF career—such as AMCHQ and Wax Museum—also occur.

Any verbiage, phrases or other references in my verses regarding the Maritimes can be easily resolved if the reader would refer to or discuss with a "Bluenose" friend. There are a number of poems regarding Canadian football. These were written over the years as an ardent football fan, for friends as ardent as myself. Many were read over the radio station before impending games by the alter-ego of a famous Canadian radio personality—Les Lye.